5

Front cover: Nevada's colorful Redrock Canyon / the
Mountain Bighorn - photograph by Roy Murphy / Alan Carey
Back cover: Alpine Lake Tahoe - photograph by Ed Cooper
Front leaf: Indian encampment at Pyramid Lake
Frontispieces in order: The Desert Bighorn - photograph
by Roy Murphy, Cathedral Gorge - photograph by James
Blank, Historic Carson Valley - photograph by Jay Aldrich.
Desert mountainscape - photograph by Roy Murphy.
Fabulous Las Vegas - photograph by Tom Campbell.
Last page: Great Basin National Park - photograph by Mark Gibson

Arrowhead Mountain
B O O K S

Written - Designed - Edited by
Adam R. Collings

Featuring the Photography of
Roy Murphy

Mechanical Production by
David Brzowski

Published in the United States
by

 ADAM RANDOLPH COLLINGS
incorporated

Box 8658 · Holiday Station
Anaheim · California · 92812

INTRODUCTION

Nevada is a land of stark contrasts-towering mountains, fertile green valleys, arid deserts, jeweled lakes, mineral-laden mines, historic ghost towns and world class resorts.

Proudly western, both in geographic location as well as in the thinking of its people, Nevada stretches across 110,540 square miles of the most remote of terrain in the continental United States. Seventh largest in the American union of states, within its boundaries is a good deal of that which comprises the very essence of the legendary American West. To the east lie the Rocky Mountains; to the west the grand Sierra Nevada. It was from the latter that the territory, and later state, got its name. Meaning ''snow-clad'' in Spanish, Nevada first appeared so named on 16th century maps of North America.

Itself corrugated by some 128 seperate mountain ranges, 86.5% of what is today the State of Nevada is owned by the United States federal government. Much of this has been designated as national forest lands, Indian reservations, military installations and, most recently, the nation's newest National Park.

A large portion of Nevada lies within what geologists refer to as the Great Basin (actually a series of some 90 basins), a vast ancient inland sea, and the only interior drainage area in the United States without rivers or waterways flowing eventually into an ocean. The Great Basin encompasses 210 square miles, measuring 880 miles long and 570 wide. The sea itself vanished in antiquity only to be brought to life again briefly at the close of the last great Ice Age (some 10,000 years ago) when run off from melting glaciers flooded much of the region. Nevada's appearance today is a reflection of the generally warmer, more arid conditions that have prevailed since that time. Even lakes which existed late enough to have been recorded on early maps have since evaporated as increasing aridity persists.

More than 150 million years of volcanic eruptions and this ebb and flow of an inland sea have created today's Nevada-one of the most geologically turbulent regions on the face of the earth, and consequently one of the richest in minerals.

As part of Alta California under Spanish, and later Mexican, rule Nevada remained literally unexplored. It was not until the gold and silver bonanzas of the middle nineteenth century that civilization's attention came to focus on this remote wilderness.

Born amidst the turmoil of Civil War, Nevada's history is one dominated by mining. At the dawning of historic times a wealth of precious metals lie vaulted beneath this untamed land. Discovery in 1864 of the fabulous Comstock with its unheard-of-wealth brought immediate respectability and gratitude to the territory from a battle-weary federal government, as silver and gold poured into the depleated coffers of the United States.

During the quarter of a century that followed granting of immediate statehood, the mines of Nevada gave rise to an opulent, extravagant lifestyle unique to the American frontier; one that continues to make itself manifest in the world-class gaming parlors and casinos of Las Vegas and Reno. Boom and bust — then boom again! Through it all Nevadans, their roots deeply-seated in the rich cultural traditions of early Mormon settlers and European emigrants, have maintained a stability at home on the ranch or farm where the excesses of the Comstock tradition are tempered by a strong agricultural economy and aggressive corporate mining operations.

Wide open country, Nevada remains the most sparsely settled region in the lower 48 states.

Today tourism/gaming, mining, and agriculture constitute the Silver State's economic bulwark. To explore this classic western frontier one but needs read on...◗

PROLOGUE

"My brother had just been appointed Secretary of Nevada Territory-an office of such majesty that it concentrated in itself the duties and dignities of Treasurer, Comptroller, Secretary of State, and Acting Governor in the Governor's absence. A salary of eighteen hundred dollars a year and the title of "Mr. Secretary," gave to the great position an air of wild and imposing grandeur. I was young and ignorant, and I envied my brother. I coveted his distinction and his financial splendor, but particularly and especially the long, strange journey he was going to make, and the curious new world he was going to explore. He was going to travel! I never had been away from home, and that word "travel" had a seductive charm for me. Pretty soon he would be hundreds and hundreds of miles away on the great plains and deserts, and among the mountains of the Far West, and would see buffaloes and Indians, and prairie-dogs, and antelopes, and have all kinds of adventures, and maybe get hanged or scalped, and have ever such a fine time, and write home and tell us all about it, and be a hero. And he would see the gold-mines and silver-mines, and maybe go about of an afternoon when his work was done, and pick up two or three pailfuls of shining slugs and nuggets of gold and silver on the hillside. And by and by he would become very rich, and return home by sea, and be able to talk as calmly about San Francisco and the ocean and "the isthmus" as if it was nothing of any consequence to have seen those marvels face to face. What I suffered in contemplating his happiness, pen cannot describe. And so, when he offered me, in cold blood, the sublime posititon of private secretary under him, it appeared to me that the heavens and the earth passed away, and the firmament was rolled together as a scroll! I had nothing more to desire. I dreamed all night about Indians, deserts, and silver bars. My contentment was complete. We were going in the overland stage from the Missouri frontier to Nevada."◗

An excerpt from Mark Twain's "Roughing It". Originally published by Harper & Brothers, New York, N.Y.

NEVADA
THE SILVER STATE

Owyhee

Jackpot

Jarbidge

95

93

Tuscarora

Midas

Wells

225

80

Winnemucca

Gerlach

Rye Patch Reservoir

Battle Mountain

Elko

Wendover

Pyramid Lake

Lovelock

278

80

305

Ruby Lake

395

Sparks
Reno

Fernley

95

Washoe Lake

Fallon

Austin

Eureka

50

Virginia City

Lake Lahontan

Incline Village

50

Ely

Lake Tahoe

Carson City

Gardnerville
Minden

Ione

Stateline

Genoa

Yerington

Walker Lake

Gabbs

376

6

93

Hawthorne

318

Pioche

Tonopah

Panaca

Goldfield

Caliente

Alamo

Rhyolite

93

Mesquite

Beatty

15

95

Overton

Pahrump

N. Las Vegas

Las Vegas

Henderson

15

Lake Mead

Boulder City

Searchlight

Lake Mojave

Laughlin

21

STATE FOSSIL

THE PREHISTORIC "ICHTHYO-SAUR" IS NEVADA'S OFFICIAL STATE FOSSIL. ICHTHYOSAURS WERE GIANT SWIMMING REP-TILES THAT INHABITED THE WORLD'S OCEANS DURING THE UPPER TRIASSIC PERIOD MORE THAN 100 MILLION YEARS AGO. THE NAME MEANS "FISH-LIZARD.TO DATE SOME 34 ICHTYOSAUR SKELETONS HAVE BEEN FOUND IN NEVADA; ALL OF THESE NEAR THE GHOST TOWN OF BERLIN IN NYE COUN-TY. THIS SITE IS NOW PART OF THE BERLIN-ICHTYOSAUR STATE PARK.

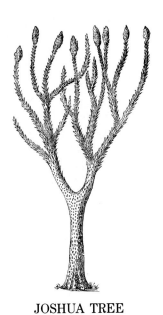

JOSHUA TREE

Regal Mt. Wheeler (preced-ing page) towers over Nevada's Great Basin National Park at 13,063 feet above the level of the sea. Photograph by Roy Murphy.

24

The American Outback, that big lonesome heart of the West. Our culture has carried on such a romance here that the rest of the world tends to see all Americans as part cowboy; a notion that is perhaps not altogether untrue. Nevada is the lean land underlying this our richest frontier myth. Born during the Age of Dinosaurs (205 million to 70 million years ago) when the Sierra Nevada, America's most formidable, unbroken chain of mountains, were formed, together with attendant gold-quartz and silver veins. Volcanos flamed and geysers spouted along this entire 400 mile-long range of mountains as gigantic plates collided beneath the earth's surface, forcing hot magma (melted rock) to well its way to the surface in spectacular, devastating, firey displays.

Towards the end of those tumultuous times, lost now in antiquity, the ocean which had covered most of the American West began retreating to its modern-day configuration. Left behind in what geologists have come to refer to as the Great Basin, was a vast, land-locked sea stranded between the granite walls of the Sierra and the stoney ramparts of the Rocky Mountains.

That sea disappeared together with the dinosaurs only to be reborn briefly following the glacial melt of the last great Ice Age.

The fossilized remains of ancient prehistoric giants testify as to the strange and varied creatures that came to inhabit this geologically turbulent region. Blocked by the Sierra Nevada, moisture from the Pacific fell only sparsely on Nevada, (average annual precipitation to this day is a meager nine inches; mountains receiving considerably more [up to 80 inches] while desert basins receive almost nothing). Albeit a harsh environment, the dramatic landscape that emerged supported a wide and varied spectrum of wildlife; ranging today from the small, inoqouis ground squirrel to the regal mountain and desert bighorn.

One of the world's great misconceptions with regards to Nevada is that it consists of nothing more than desert wasteland, sand dunes, and alkali flats. In actuality the Silver State, as Nevada has come to be called, sports spectacular alpine scenery, hill country, high plains, as well as the most varied and extensive desert country in North America.

Correspondingly, plant life here too is extremely diverse, being divided roughly into two main categories; desert vegetation and alpine vegetation; with a broad, sweeping middle area where the two converge.

Most striking among Nevada's desert vegetation is the Joshua tree, oddly enough a member of the lily family sporting a bushy, tree-like top. Prehistoric and imposing, the Joshua tree was so named by early Mormon settlers to whom its arms out-stretched towards heaven reminded them of the biblical character in the Old Testament who suceeded the prophet Moses in Israel.

Sage covers the vast majority of Nevada's Great Basin terrain, so much so as to have been recognized as the Silver State's flower. It does infact sport tiny white or yellow blossoms during late spring and early summer.

Among much of the hill country is one of Nevada's two officially designated state trees, the pinyon pine. Usually eight to fifteen feet tall, rare specimens actually attain a height of up to fifty feet. Dark green, with single-leaf, aromatic needles, knarled branches, and purple-brown cones, the pinyon pine is famed for its seeds (pine nuts), which, when gathered and roasted, made up a major dietary staple for the native American Indians.

Aspens and cottonwoods (both decidious trees) grow in profusion along streams and rivers.

Ponderosa and Jeffrey pine, red fir and alpine (white) fir adorn the high country. At timberline Nevada's second state tree, the ancient bristlecone (oldest living thing on earth) braves true alpine conditions in a hostile environment. Bristlecone have been known to live for more than 4,000 years.

BOBCAT

VALLEY OF FIRE

ROY MURPHY

It was during the last great Ice Age, some 25,000 years ago, when man first arrived in Nevada. This oldest known Southwest civilization, referred to by anthropologists as the Desert Culture, were nomadic hunters, who came in pursuit of herds of big game. Those who settled in the Great Basin region developed an extensive network of city- states, and came to be known collectively as the Anasazi. Most impressive of the Anasazi settlements in Nevada was Pueblo Grande, an intermitent village stretching 30 miles along the Muddy River northeast of present day Las Vegas. Here the Anasazi reached its zenith. Excelling in pottery making, basketry, domestication of animals, and agriculture, they built grand adobe buildings and complex irrigation systems. Then suddenly, around the year 1150 AD, they simply disappeared. One of the great mysteries of the Southwest, anthropologists can only speculate as to what became of these most noble ''savages'', whose civilization rivaled that of even the Mayan.

By the time Europeans ''discovered'' Nevada they found only adobe ruins and scattered tribes of semi-nomadic Indians - the Washoe, Shoshone, Northern and Southern Paiutes - whose primitive cultures and traditions were far removed from those of their ''civilized'' ancestors.

Today Indian art in the form of petroglyphs and rock paintings, unique cave dwellings and adobe ruins are scattered across the rock-ribbed mountains and valleys of the Silver State.

ROY MURPHY

ANASAZI POTTERY

GRIMES POINT PETROGLYPHS

LEGEND OF THE PINYON PINE

The external struggle between good and evil is told in the legends of the Washoe, who still relate how the good Wolf God tried to preserve Carson Valley as an ''Eden'' and how the wicked Coyote God debauched the tribe.

The Wolf God directed a prehistoric river north past Job's Peak, and taught the Washoes to bathe in it, cleansing away all sin and disease, and gaining immortality. Paiutes, Shoshones, and Diggers came from points later called Bodie, Mason Valley, Walker River and Pyramid, and they came as friends, dancing, feasting, singing. Fish, deer, and rabbits were plentiful and there was no pain or sickness.

But Gou-Wet, the Coyote God, who is the devil of the Washoes, taught them evil ways, warning them their hands would become like his; they would become old and die; they would forget how to make bows, arrows, and hunt, and in time he would eat them...with that warning, he won them to licentious ways of evil. And soon all game disappeared and there was no food, no warm rabbit robes. The babies cried from cold, and sickness came. The Paiutes made war and took all the ponies. The Washoes had been many but now they died and the tribe dwindled in size. Then the pine nut forests were destroyed by fire.

Bitterly the Washoes reflected if it had not been for the Coyote God they would have been immortal and numerous. But their friend the Wolf God had not forsaken them. Out of pity he made vast numbers of hunting arrowheads and cast them over the land. But the cunning Coyote God poisoned them so that any unwary Washoe who picked them up died a lingering death. (To this day, a Washoe believes it very unlucky to pick up an arrowhead with the point toward him.)

Again the Wolf God tried to help his friends, this time scattering pine nuts which sprang magically into forests. But the Washoes were so weak with hunger they could not reach the pine nuts on the trees. Again the Wolf God came to the rescue and he started to strike the pinon pines on the tops, making dwarfs of the trees so the Washoes could gather the cones. Desperately the Coyote God wheedled, and argued, and talked, trying to get the Wolf God to stop shrinking the nut pines. Every trick, every argument, every enticement he could devise, the Coyote God tried, but the Wolf God remained firm. He shrank thousands of nut pine trees and the hungry Washoes harvested the crop and were saved.

And ever since, the Washoes have depended on the pine nut for food, and the pine nut trees have obeyed the Wolf God, and remained short; so the Washoes, young and old, strong and weak, rich and poor, could harvest the nuts with ease.

The Catholic monarchs of Spain were the first Europeans to lay claim to Nevada by virture of their conquest of Mexico in 1519, and subsequent voyage of Juan Rodriguz Cabrillo to the California coast. Missions and settlements were established in Arizona, Texas, New Mexico, and much later in California. It was this latest settlement of what the Spanish referred to as Alta California that brought the first Europeans to Nevada territory. Iberian explorers came within miles of present day state boundaries as they ventured into both the High Sierra and the Sonora Desert, but none actually entered Nevada until the year 1776 when Captain Juan Bautista de Anza, in company with Father Francisco Hermenegildo Garces, in search of a convenient route between the missions of Arizona and those being established in California, traversed present day Clark County.

The Spanish Trail, as their route came to be known would, during the years ahead, serve as a major thoroughfare across the American Southwest, much of it paralleled today by a highly sophisticated network of highways and interstate freeway systems.

It was the belief of many Spanish colonials that a great river, referred to as Rio San Buenaventura, bisected Nevada territory, flowing westward to California. No such river existed. A misunderstanding between Indian and Spaniard, a fanciful stroke of the pen by an inventive European cartographer; whatever the reason, the myth of this legendary river persisted for several hundred years. Garces and Anza were only the first of many reputable explorers and frontiersmen who sought it out. John Charles Fremont would search for it in 1843. Had such a river existed it would have been of tremendous value as a trade route. Regardless, there was no such waterway.

By virture of the change of command in Mexico City, following that country's successful revolution for independence from Spain, Nevada became Mexican territory in 1821. Still void of European settlement the Nevada frontier remained primitive and pristine.

Fierce competition for beaver pelts between British trappers of the famed Hudson's Bay Company and American mountain men working for the Rocky Mountain and American Fur Companies pushed the boundaries of the American frontier ever westward.

First to enter the Silver State was one Jedediah Strong Smith, a frontiersman well respected for his literacy and religious ethics. Smith's integrity and courage earned him part ownership in the Rocky Mountain Fur Company. As a partner he set out to locate and harvest new beaver populations. Jed's subsequent explorations led to his accolade "the greatest pathfinder of the American West."

In 1826 Smith's wanderings brought him to Southern Nevada. He found no pelts to harvest. Leaving the Colorado River he pushed westward into California, returning later the

STATE ANIMAL

THE DESERT BIGHORN (OVIS CANADENSIS NELSONI) IS NEVADA'S OFFICIAL STATE ANIMAL. IT IS SMALLER THAN ITS ROCKY MOUNTAIN COUSIN BUT HAS A WIDER SPREAD OF HORNS. THE BIGHORN IS WELL-SUITED FOR NEVADA'S MOUNTAINOUS DESERT COUNTRY BECAUSE IT CAN GO FOR LONG PERIODS WITHOUT WATER.
THE BIGHORN SUBSISTS ON GRASS, PINE NUTS, WILD BUSHES, AND SOMETIMES EVEN MORMON TEA, YUCCA, JOSHUA AND CACTUS PLANTS.
LARGE RAMS STAND ABOUT THREE-AND-A-HALF FEET HIGH AND AVERAGE 160 POUNDS BUT CAN WEIGH AS MUCH AS 250. EWES AVERAGE ABOUT 100 POUNDS.
THE DESERT BIGHORN IS CONSIDERED THE RAREST AND MOST HIGHLY PRIZED OF NORTH AMERICA'S BIG GAME.

SAHWAVE MOUNTAINS

BENJAMIN L.E. BONNEVILLE

following year by crossing the Sierra Nevada, the first white man ever to do so. From Ebbetts Pass he descended into what is now central Nevada and traversed the state, returning to rendevous with his men in Salt Lake.

Chartered in London in 1668, the Hudson's Bay Company had established trading ventures with the Indian nations of North America long before the days of the American Revolution. In an effort to maintain superiority over such American competition as that posed by Jedediah Smith, the British contracted with one Peter Skene Ogden, a man as at home in elegant London as he was around the campfire of his Indian Wives, to lead their trapping expeditions into the as yet untried territories of the American Southwest, and this without the blessing of the newly founded Mexican government.

Ogden had a well earned reputation for being able to outdrink, outswear, and outbrawl any man on the western frontier with a penchant for quoting the Bible and Shakespeare to his men. In 1826 he boldly breeched Mexican law and provoked Indian hostilities when he guided his trapper troops into the forever reaches of northeastern Nevada. These expeditions subsequently led him across the state no less than eight times by the year 1830.

Trained for the law, Peter's successful ventures in the field served to strengthen his position with company ownership

ROY MURPHY

in Great Britian. Ogden was advanced to head up the Hudson's Bay Company which he did affectively until his death at the age of 60 in 1854.

ollowing in the footsteps of trailblazers Jed Smith and Peter Ogden came Captain Joseph Redeford Walker. A french-born, American army officer, Redeford had been successful in opening up the Rocky Mountain area to fur traders. In 1833, in company with Captain Benjamin Louis Eulalie de Bonneville, Walker followed Humboldt River out in to Nevada's high plains, all the way to the base of the Sierra. First to enter present day Carson Valley (site of modern day Nevada's state capitol) he pushed across the High Sierra, this in the dead of winter, to discover Yosemite Valley, and California's giant Sierra redwoods. What he did not discover was the fictitious San Buenaventura River. Bonneville's book, published by Washington Irving in 1837, attempted to lay to rest any lingering belief in its supposed existence.

Walker went on to gain notoriety in California as a pioneer, entrepreneur and statesman.

JOSEPH REDEFORD WALKER

33

GREAT BASIN NATIONAL PARK

The ageless rock of the Great Basin has been tormented and twisted for over 600 million years. Today a dusty, volcanic dish claiming most all of present-day Nevada, its most arrogant feature is 13,063 foot Wheeler Peak.

In the upper reaches of this singular mountain one encounters alpine lakes, tundra and forests of ancient bristlecone pine. In the shadow of its peak lies America's southern-most glacier, a 20,000-year-old remnant of the Ice Age.

Beneath this wild and remote masif are sur-realistic caverns filled with stalactites, stalagmites, helictites, shields, and draperies.

Such attributes were considered by congress to be so unique that in 1986 77,000 acres surrounding Wheeler Peak were designated as Great Basin National Park. America's 49th such park it was dedicated one year later on the one hundreth birthday celebration of Yellowstone, the world's first National Park.

CHRISTOPHER "KIT" CARSON

JOHN CHARLES FREMONT

Underwritten by the United States Congress, who were determined to get to the bottom of the San Buenaventura River issue, John Charles Fremont came west at the head of an extensive mapping party. Departing the east in 1843 he and his men spent 4 years exploring the American frontier. His "top secret" work provided much valuable information to "aid" the United States in "liberating" California from the Mexicans.

It was Fremont's second expedition in 1845 that gave us one of the most important maps in the history of the west. Together with Kit Carson he successfully charted the entirety of America's Southwest, giving to a restless American populace their first actual map of this previously untried wilderness.

One of the most influential, and certainly controversial men in western history, Fremont would go on to serve as governor of California, US Senator from California, unsuccessful Republican presidential candidate, Western Department Army Commander during the Civil War, and Arizona Territorial Governor.

Fremont's companion, Christopher "Kit" Carson is heralded as having been second only to Daniel Boone as the greatest hero of the American Frontier. Kit ran away at 16 from a saddlers apprenticeship to become a caravan boy and fur trapper. He would later take two Indian wives before marrying the beautiful 15 year old Josepha Jaramillo, a young woman, well-born, of California aristocracy.

Undefeatable as an Indian-fighter and scalp-taker, renowned as a buffalo hunter, short and stocky, Kit Carson was christened "Little Chief" by the Indians. He gained fame as Fremont's guide upon publication of articles about the Captain's explorations and adventures. It was Fremont who named river, mountain pass, and valley in honor of his friend. In 1858 Kit would be further honored when Nevada's Carson City was laid out and named after the famed frontiersman.

Rejected by the US Senate in 1848 for a lieutenancy in the army due to his illiteracy, Carson served as an army guide and worked his ranch until being appointed as Indian Agent at Taos, New Mexico in 1853. It was there that he died in 1868 at the age of 59.

In 1838 the first recorded overland emigration of Americans to California traversed the vast high plains of northern Nevada. Abandoning wagons and household goods at the foot of the mountains they made a desperate attempt to make it over the High Sierra.

A splinter group of this, what has come to be known as the Bidwell-Bartlesen party, headed south to Las Vegas Meadows, then on to Southern California in an effort to avoid the treacherous Sierra crossing. All arrived safely prompting other anxious adventurers to risk the difficult journey and head west.

By 1845 more than 250 covered wagons had traversed Nevada enroute to California. Most tragic was that of the Donner Party which, when trapped by winter snows in the high mountain pass that to this day bares their name, resorted to cannibalism in a desperate effort to survive.

During the decade that followed the number of emigrants in a single party had mounted to three thousand, the Emigrant Trail across Nevada territory well worn and repeatedly marked by abandoned wagons, animal skeletons and primitive graves.

Following the close of the war with Mexico in 1848 and the subsequent discovery of gold in California an endless stream of wagon trains made their way west to the Sierra gold fields. Nevada remained a mere obstacle to be overcome before reaching the fabled west coast land of milk and honey. As such, settlement of the territory was not considered; that is until the Church of Jesus

ALONG THE EMIGRANT TRAIL (BELOW)

DUNE MOUNTAIN

Christ of Latter Day Saints, more commonly referred to as the Mormons, set up headquarters in adjacent Utah territory in July of 1847 after having been driven from the United States by lynch mobs and unbridled prejudice. Following expulsion from New York, Ohio, Missouri and Illinois for a variety of reasons, all steeped in religious intolerance (a most unlikely scenario in view of the fact that this was an American incident), the Mormons saw in this land that no one else wanted-the very place where they could forge their lives out of harms way. Dangers were many but when compared to the hatred they had faced in the United States Indian savages and grizzly bears seemed manageable challenges.

Prophet and leader of the fledging religion, Brigham Young laid claim to the whole of Utah and Nevada (and to much of Arizona and Southern California as well). The vision of his people was to establish an empire that would be economically self-sufficient while at the same time expansive enough to assimilate the thousands of new converts arriving daily from Europe and the United States. They called their "nation" the State of Deseret. Young immediately set about colonizing.

BRIGHAM YOUNG

ROY MURPHY

JAY ALDRICH

MORMON STATION

SAGE GROUSE

In 1849 a Mormon trading post was established in the Carson Valley at present-day Genoa, Nevada. Success ensued as trail-weary emigrants swapped spent horses and cattle together with burdensome household goods for fresh animals and sorely needed supplies on this, the last leg of their journey to California. Nevertheless the project was abandoned as per Young's instructions only to be re-established permanently in 1851 by Mormon entrepreneurs excited about the proven profitabilty of the enterprise. This, the first true settlement of the Nevada territory, thus ushered in a colorful pagaentry of human history.

In the site of present day Genoa, traditionally a winter camp for the Washo Indians, Mormon Elder John Reese constructed a 30 by 50 foot combination hotel and store within the confines of a secure stockade. Mormon Station, as it came to be called, experienced immediate success and continued to do so for many years.

Only days after their arrival the LDS (Latter Day Saints as the Mormons called themselves) Mott family settled to the south of Genoa, establishing the town of Mottsville. To the

GENOA

JAY ALDRICH

north a half dozen Mormon Elders, back from the California Gold Rush, established the Eagle Valley Ranch. All met with financial success.

In 1851 Nevada was included as Utah Territory by the Federal Government. As part of the unoffical State of Deseret, disgruntled non-mormon settlers arriving in the Carson Valley, at the time Nevada's only settled territory, petitioned for annexation from Utah territory to the state of California in an effort to avoid domination by the LDS "theocracy in the wilderness". Their appeals went unanswered.

The next town to be established in present-day Nevada was called Franktown in adjacent Washoe Valley. The year was 1854, just shortly after Carson County had been created out of what was still designated as Utah Territory and after Mormon Orsen Hyde, an apostle of the LDS Church, had been appointed probate judge by territorial Governor Brigham Young.

Judge Hyde had cleverly arranged for the election day of Carson County officials to fall after enough Mormons could arrive from Salt Lake to dominate the vote.

Hyde redesigned Reese's Mormon Station, offically naming it Genoa, and encourged the further development of Franktown (which would later preceed San Francisco as the site of the first Western Stock Exchange).

Subsequent colonies were established in the Muddy River Valley and Meadow Valley regions of Nevada.

IN THE NEAR DISTANCE LOOM THE TURRETS AND MINARETS OF THE RUBY MOUNTAINS, GREEN IN SUMMER, SNOW-BURIED IN WINTER, AND SPLASHED IN AUTUMN WITH ENTIRE HILLSIDES OF GOLDEN ASPEN. AT THEIR BASE LIES THE HAMLET OF lAMOILLE, WHICH IN PIONEER DAYS WAS A DETOUR TRAIL WHEN FEED GREW SCARCE ALONG THE HUMBOLDT RIVER.

41

In 1855 Mormon Elder William Bringhurst formed a settlement at Las Vegas Meadows in present day Clark County. For years this remained Nevada's only settlement outside of the Carson Valley area. Bringhurst, as it was originally called when the first post office was opened there, continued as a successful trading post on the Salt Lake - Los Angeles (Mission San Gabriel) Trail and later served as headquarters for a Mormon mission to the Indians.

Mail service remained irregular at best between California's Capitol of Sacramento, the Mormon Capitol at Salt Lake and Nevada's Colonies. Mormon and non-Mormon, their ties either with the Golden State or the Mormon State of Deseret, forged working farms and ranches out of the isolated frontier. Logging and mining operations were begun in earnest, while trading with the thousands making their way to either the gold fields or Los Angeles kept a continual flux of goods and monies flowing into the territory.

Relations between Mormon officials and non-Mormon federal authorities in Utah had never been good. In the Nevada Colonies "Gentiles (non- Mormons)" would often disrupt LDS community functions; drunken, abusive, and looking for women. Having tolerated such abuses for more than a decade in the United States, Latter-Day Saints had since become the type of Christians that were not so readily willing to "turn the other cheek". In Deseret "they" were in charge. This coupled by the fact that Mormons were infact deliberately attempting to control the territory led to a declaration of war against them.

Exaggerated reports, instigated by those anxious to weaken the Mormon domination of the west, made their way to the nation's capitol where legislators were led to believe that the people of Utah territory were in a "state of rebellion."

Subsequently Washington D.C. declared war against the Mormon State of Deseret. The United States Army was sent west to squelch a non- existent rebellion. Brigham Young called all Mormon settlers to return to Salt Lake at once.

Carson Valley and Las Vegas pioneers were forced to give away their hard-earned farms and ranches to anxious non-Mormons, divesting themselves of all worldy riches to obey the words of their prophet.

Subsequently there was no effective government in the Nevada settlements. The non-existent rebellion in Utah was resolved, yet Mormons did not return in any great numbers, choosing instead to strenghten their ranks closer to the security of church headquarters at Salt Lake City.

MORMON TEMPLE

"OH, THE MORMON ROSES AND THE MORMON POPLARS! WHEREVER THE MORMONS WENT, THEY PLANTED. WHEREVER THEY HAD BEEN, THERE ROSES BLOOM."

VIRGINIA CITY

From the very outset Virginia City displayed an eager appetite for entertainment. Hardly was the rush to the Comstock well underway before a theatre was constructed in this newly-born, rough-and-tumble city. That was in 1860, and almost before the first one was completed, two more theatres were erected. Within three years the town's entertainment had become as fabulous as the lode itself. At one time five different companies were playing nightly to packed houses, presenting anything and everything in drama from Shakespeare on down the list and, as if this wasn't enough, six additional variety shows were packing overflow audiences into tent pavilions with song and dance routines.

Virginia City had reached its zenith...the Comstock became the cultural capital of the West...a reputation that even San Francisco couldn't dispute for two decades!

Piper's Opera House was in no little way responsible for Virginia City's entertainment fame. Across its stage, managed by David Belasco, the great and near great passed in review before the appreciative eyes of Comstock theatre goers. From its flickering footlights the golden voice of Adelina Patti held listeners spellbound; down its sloping boards General Tom Thumb and his diminutive wife walked toward a thunderous roar of approval and found Virginia City at their feet. Others had their triumph here too, Edwin Booth, Clara Morris, James O'Neill, Frank Mayo, Madame Modjeska to name but a few. Such plays as "East Lynne," "Davey Crockett," "Under the Gaslight," and a long series of Shakespearian renditions were common diet for theatre goers. But, accustomed to the best the stage had to offer, even Virginia City gasped at daring Adah Menken!

If Adah had astounded San Francisco, she certainly succeeded in amazing Virginia City, but Virginia City loved amusement! Ladies tittered and blushed behind their fluttering fans and the men leaned forward in their seats when Adah appeared in Mazeppa riding a horse across the stage of Piper's Opera House. It wasn't the horse that caused excitement, but Adah herself, for in this daring scene she was clad in pink tights! Her startling departure from the accepted mode of stage dress was comparable to the fan dance or strip tease of half a century later.

Virginia City loved it, and to show proper appreciation the camp presented Adah Menken with a bar of bullion worth two thousand dollars. Virginia City and later historians have made much of the "cultural recreation" available on the Comstock, but the intense young people on Sun Mountain were impatient for quick fortunes, and truth was, they loved the colorful and the sensational. Today this tradition lives on in the showrooms of Nevada's gaming resorts.

MAJOR ORMSBY

ABRAHAM CURRY

nnoticed by the LDS community, would-be shopkeeper, Abraham Curry, had arrived in the Mormon Colony of Genoa in 1852 where he pronounced commercial store lots overpriced and vowed to build his own town. With his resources he arranged to purchase the Eagle Valley Ranch. Together with several partners he proceeded to lay out a town site. Subsequently sold to, Major William M. Ormsby, Curry's rival community became Carson City, and would go on to serve as the capital city of the future state.

In June of 1859 Captain James H. Simpson, topographical engineer for two wagon routes between Nevada territories Genoa and the Mormon Capitol of Salt Lake, passed through Carson City. He described it as having two stores (one of which was Major Ormsby's) and about a dozen small houses.

By this time Curry was involved in another venture, that of establishing the Warm Springs Hotel, subsequent meeting place of the first Nevada Territorial Legislature in late 1861.

Abraham Curry would go on to invest in a mining venture that would ultimately inaugurate the Silver Bonanza of the Comstock Lode, being the first to discover large quantities of silver ore in the territory.

Three of the principal players in the discovery of the fabulous Comstock were probably quietly working Nevada's Gold Canyon at the time John Reese established Mormon Station in 1851. James Finney, or Ol' Virginney as his friends called him, was said to have met Reese there and later worked for Reese as a teamster. The two Grosch brothers were also working the Canyon at that time. Ethan Allan Grosch, together with one Hosea Ballou, among the first all-year placer miners in Nevada, staked a claim, the Pioneer, on the very ledge where the famed Orphir Mine was subsequently discovered. Neither lived to see any gain from their enterprise; both dieing of blood poisoning in 1857 (Hosea from a pick injury in the spring of the year and Ethan the following November after refusing amputation of his frozen feet to save his life in the Sierra).

When "bluestuff" was found by these first Nevada gold prospectors, as they worked their way up the canyons towards Mount Davidson, it was considered a nuisance. Then some one realized that the "nuisance" was in fact fabulously rich silver.

Frequent gold and silver strikes made it apparent to those few present that Nevada's eastern Sierra foothills held a bonanza to rival that of California's western Sierra gold fields. Subsequently the first offical mining district in what was still considered Utah territory, the Virginia Mining District was inaugurated by James "Ol' Virginney" Finney, on a larger vein of gold west of the as yet untapped Comstock. The year was 1858.

In 1859 news of success in Nevada mining ventures reached the West Coast. The Forty-niners of California's gold rush retraced their steps back across the Sierra to the bypassed bonanzas of Nevada's gold and silver mines.

Ol' Virginney himself would go on to christen Virginia City when in a drucken spree he fell, broke his bottle, and loathe to waste a single drop pronounced "I baptize this ground Virginia".

NEVADA
THE SILVER STATE

ROY MURPHY

 eportedly it was John Jessup who orignally discovered the fabulous Ophir Mine. He managed to get himself murdered shortly thereafter. Payment in 1864 was made by the Ophir of $30,000 to Jessup's mother for his claim, said to be the first filed on what would soon be referred to as the Comstock.

On the scene since 1863 was one Henry Thomas Paige Comstock, a fur trapper-turned prospector. Famed for introducing sourdough bread (a staple among Forty-Niners) to many a miner, he became known as "Old Pancake." This legendary mountain man was about to be thrown into the limelight of fame and fortune.

Some say that Peter O'Rilley and Patrick Mc Laughlin, emigrants from Ireland, sold the Ophir claim (the artful frontier crime of claim jumping) while the majority of area residents were away at the Eagle Valley Ranch to hear an indictment for the murder of Jesup brought against one William Sides. Others say that the Irish partners laid illegitimate claim to the Ophir by virture of their discovery of the silver while digging a well at the head of Six Mile Canyon.

Regardless Henry Comstock happened along to convince the two that he had inherited the land from the Grosches. Thus he and a friend, Emanuel Penrod, were listed on the location notice together with O'Riley, Mc Laughlin and "Ol' Virginney", whose share was subsequently acquired by

HYDRAULIC MINING

JAMES BLANK

THE CASTLE

JOHN McKAY

WILLIAM O'BRIEN

Comstock in trade for a horse and bottle of whiskey.

On August 30, 1859 Penrod, Comstock & Company shipped its first load of silver ore from the Ophir to San Francisco where it brought $3,000 a ton.

Unlike placer (gold) mining, where one man could work on a rocker alone, running water through a sluice box to wash the dirt from the gold ore, extracting silver from the mines, was an expensive proposition. It often required the taking on of partners to provide necessary capital. The levying of assessments for working capital often squeezed out partners. Such was the case with Penrod who sold, fearing assessment, and O'Riley who sold to one John O. Earl and Judge James Walsh a month or so after Mc Laughlin sold in September to the George Hearst interests, each for a few thousand dollars. In most of the first claims on what would become known as the Comstock Lode the original claim holders sold out within months, with Comstock, probably coming into use to describe this flurry of share transfers.

As more and more ore was discovered the cry went up "On to the Comstock", much to Henry's delight.

espite the severity of the winter of 1859-60 some 10,000 hopeful prospectors rushed to the Comstock. Mines sprang up like mushrooms after rain a mere ten foot claim often proving worth a fortune as Sandy and Eilley (Allison) Bowers would demonstrate by virture of their subsequent gigantic European spending spree. Sandy Bower's mine was yielding as much as $100,000 in silver ore a month.

Mexican miners introduced a massive grinding mill, which they called an arrastre to break up the ore. Yankee prospectors replaced the burro powered operation, a slow prospect at best, with steam-powered quartz mills. Soon some 76 such mills were in operation.

By her first birthday, in 1860, Virginia City boasted a hotel, nine restaurants, 42 saloons, bathhouse, ten laundries, tailor and dressmaker, two barbers, a dentist, seven cobblers, ten stables, seven blacksmiths, a surveyor, five brokers, 38 general stores and one school to serve some 2400 miners.

It was at about this time that one John McKay arrived upon the scene. His career began as an Irish miner turned partner

in what proved to be the richest strike on the Comstock. William O'Brien arrived with McKay, to work in the mines. Like his comrade he would become one of Nevada's most powerful silver magnates.

Amidst the 18 competing newspapers reporting Nevada's suddenly frenzied state of affairs was the now famous Territorial Enterprise which arrived upon the scene in 1860.

Nevada's silver boom along the Comstock fueled the continued expansion of the West just as California's gold rush began to wane. Its effects would further enhance the extravagant growth of San Francisco as a major finanical center, strengthing the North in the face of eminent Civil War against the South, and bringing immediate territorial status and later statehood to Nevada itself.

Mansions were built, cultural hallmarks (among them an opera house),and churches rose from the sage covered foothills of the Eastern Sierra. Adjacent Aurora, Virginia City's rival, flourished. The era of the Comstock was in full swing.

ith hundreds of prospectors and settlers pouring into Nevada's Carson and Washoe Valleys, lured by news of the fabulous Comstock, the traditional peace-loving Indians of the region faced conflict and confrontation from all sides. Many American emigrants came from areas of Indian Wars in the midwest, bringing with them prejudice unbefitting the tribes of the Sierra and high desert. Ready to believe any report of savagery by the "redskins" the native Americans faced a no-win situation with regards to this "invasion" enmasse of Western civilization.

In the Spring of 1860 two young Pauite women were abducted by Yankee traders. Confined to a cabin, they were subsequently located by their tribe who avenged the women by killing their abductors. Word of the incident reached Carson City where Major William Ormsby organized a militia of one hundred-plus Carson City rangers to squelch the "savages". A more ridiculous scenario than that which occured, when viewed from afar with today's prespective, could not have played itself out.

Numaga, "war leader" of the Pauite, awaited his assailants, prepared to defend the rights and supremacy of his people. At Pyramid Lake the Indians annihilated the whites, killing

"YOU WOULD MAKE WAR UPON THE WHITES. I ASK YOU TO PAUSE AND REFLECT. THE WHITE MEN ARE LIKE THE STARS OVER YOUR HEADS. YOU HAVE WRONGS, GREAT WRONGS, THAT RISE UP LIKE THOSE MOUNTAINS BEFORE YOU. BUT CAN YOU, FROM THE MOUNTAIN-TOPS, REACH AND BLOT OUT THOSE STARS? YOUR ENEMIES ARE LIKE THE SANDS IN THE BEDS OF YOUR OWN RIVERS. WHEN TAKEN AWAY THEY ONLY GIVE PLACE FOR MORE TO COME AND SETTLE THERE COULD YOU DEFEAT THE WHITES OF NEVADA, FROM OVER THE MOUNTAINS IN CALIFORNIA WOULD COME TO HELP THEM AN ARMY OF WHITE MEN THAT WOULD COVER YOUR COUNTRY LIKE A BLANKET. WHAT HOPE IS THERE FOR THE PAH-UTE? FROM WHERE IS TO COME YOUR GUNS, YOUR POWDER, YOUR LEAD, YOUR DRIED MEATS TO LIVE UPON, AND HAY TO FEED YOUR PONIES WITH WHILE YOU CARRY ON THIS WAR? YOUR ENEMIES HAVE ALL OF THESE THINGS, MORE THAN THEY CAN USE. THE WILL COME LIKE THE SAND IN A WHIRLWIND AND DRIVE YOU FROM YOUR HOMES. YOU WILL BE FORCED AMONG THE BAR-REN ROCKS OF THE NORTH, WHERE YOUR PONIES WILL DIE; WHERE YOU WILL SEE THE WOMEN AND OLD MEN STARVE, AND LISTEN TO THE CRIES OF YOUR CHILDREN FOR FOOD. I LOVE MY PEOPLE; LET THEM LIVE; AND WHEN THEIR SPIRITS SHALL BE CALLED TO THE GREAT CAMP IN THE SOUTHERN SKY, LET THEIR BONES REST WHERE THEIR FATHERS WERE BURIED."

—CHIEF NUMAGA

Ormsby along with most of his rangers in what proved to be the bloodiest massacre in Nevada's history.

Yet despite their momentary victory the fate of the native Americans had long since been sealed. A few days later some 500 men backed by 200 Army regulars returned to the site. There they erected Fort Churchill - the ultimate act of domination by the white man in Indian territory. With this military installation of weapon supremacy in their midst, the Pauite were forced into submission, unable to stand up to the many offenses continually commited against them. Few skirmishes followed.

Fort Churchill, Nevada's first and most important military installation, was but the vanguard for a complete invasion of the territory by the United States Government. Some 35 camps, forts and reservations were subsequently established throughout Nevada territory by the federal government between 1860 and 1880.

Against the abuses inflicted upon Nevada Indians rose the voice of Sarah Winnemucca, daughter of Winnemucca II and sister of Natchez, who became famous as "the Pauite Princess" when she began lecturing on the desperate plight of her starving people after years of fruitless protests to the United States Federal Government.

A magnificent woman, born in the 1840's to share a childhood with white Nevada yet educated only briefly, Sarah served first as an interpreter for Indian agents and later as both army guide and scout.

Writing about the plight of her people brought the long awaited response from Washington where she was called upon to establish the first American all-Indian school in an attempt to balance the inequities between Indian and whites in the West.

In 1881 the school opened on Sarah's brother's farm near Lovelock.

Sarah's continued efforts on behalf of her people led to passage of the Davis Act in 1887, making it posssible for Indians to become American citizens.

Fort Churchill's adobe buildings would bring only $750 at an 1890 auction before it was leased as a ranch. Today a state park, some of its structures have since been restored.

---

 lbeit one of the briefest chapters in the history of the American West, that of the Pony Express was certainly one of the most romantic-courageous young men racing across the Great West from "St Joseph Missouri to Sacramento, California astride the swiftest and strongest ponies in a record ten days time, all while braving desperados, Indians, blizzards, duststorms and floods (in winter the same 2,000 mile trip was extended to 15 days).

The service was said to have started with a boast made in Washington D.C. by one William Russell of Russell, Majors & Waddel who bet $10,000 that he could get the mail from Missouri to California in ten days, a feat Major George Chorpenning had been unable to match in filling his mail

CHIEF NUMAGA

ROY MURPHY

contract since 1851. Chorpenning's Butterfield Stagecoach Lines were carrying mail via a southern route through El Paso, Texas.

Advertising for "young, small, strong orphans" as riders, Russell, Majors, & Waddel laid out some 200 stations along a 2,000 mile route, of which almost 500 traversed present day Nevada (from Fridays Station just east of the California State line to Antelope Springs Station just west of the present Utah border).

The first riders did 30 to 50 miles a day on three horses, with two minute change-of-horses time alotted, for $50 a month, plus mount.

Later, distances for riders were extended to up to 70 and 100 miles per run, horses being as carefully selected as riders. In some cases bonuses of up to $150 monthly were paid for braving extra hazards such as Indian attacks, outlaw holdup

JIGGS RANCH

attempts, winter storms, etc.

Although the speed and continuous run records of one Egan for a 330- mile non-stop ride and of young William ''Buffalo Bill'' Cody for a 322- mile dash under hazardous conditions are often quoted, Nevada's Robert ''Pony Bob'' Haslam was said to have made a non-stop 190-mile run across Nevada and then the return 190-mile ride without so much as a nap.

Most famous run of all was that of March 1861, when riders carrying Lincoln's inaugural address made the entire distance in seven days and seventeen hours.

Although a financial failure, the glory of the Pony Express will live on forever. From inception in April of 1860 until its termination a mere 18 months later at the linking of transcontinental telegraph lines, the Pony Express served as a lifeline to civilization on an isolated frontier.

''THE BIG LONESOME, NEVADA IS SAGEBRUSH COUNTRY, WITH SOME NINE SAGEBRUSH SPECIES AND 18 SUBSPECIES HOLDING THE DESERT BASINS IN PLACE.''

The Comstock would have great, far-reaching, and lasting effects in the history of both Nevada and the nation. Strikes would continue off and on for several decades with towns shifting locations like Hollywood movie sets.

Comstock miners were completely dependant upon freight companies both for needed supplies as well as for a means by which to get their ore to the mint. Consequently toll roads and mule team operators "mined" as much from the pockets of the prospectors as any successful miner took from the Comstock itself.

Tiny Genoa boomed once again, this time as a commerical shipping and social center, Carson City as focal point for aspiring politicians, while Virginia City maintained her preeminence as Queen of the Comstock.

By 1863 the Queen of the Comstock had become the second largest city in the West, this at a time when it seemed as if silver would forever flow freely from her mines. Yet the Big Bonanza didn't come until 10 years later when the Consolidated Virginia Mine yielded an unprecendented $100 million in silver ore. Although momentary, it was then that Virginia City became the richest city in the world.

Captain John C. Fremont is credited for having "discovered" spectacular Lake Tahoe on February 14th 1844. Lost in snowdrifts, his men having been reduced to eating their mules in a desperate attempt to survive the treacherous winter crossing, Fremont was so moved by what he saw that in the midst of such despair he found himself extolling in his journal upon the beauty of this vast "Lake of the Sky." "So entirely surrounded by mountains," wrote the captain, "we could not determine its full extent."

Frontier journalist Mark Twain, working out of Virginia City, would later sing the praise of this alpine wonder when he reported, "The clear blue waters blended so with the blue sky overhead that a man in a boat had the sensation of floating in air."

Located at 6,228 feet above sea level with an actual length of 21.6 miles and a width of 12 miles Tahoe is, in fact, of glacial origin, its vastness drained by the Truckee River. Indian for, simply enough "lake", Tahoe is surrounded by the 10,000 foot crest of the High Sierra, presenting a truly spectacular setting.

At the beginning of the silver boom on the Comstock, Lake Tahoe remained remote and pristine. There was, in fact, a pony express and stage remount station, Friday's Station, along its South Shore, and a lone sawmill stood a few miles distant at present-day Glenbrook.

The subsequent explosion of mining activity at the base of the mountain was to fuel unprecedented logging activity however. Subsequently within a few short years Lake Tahoe became the epicenter of a timber baron's dream. By 1815 a narrow-gauge railroad was carrying both logs and passengers up and down the Sierra while more than a dozen sawmills screeched away both night and day.

FELLING A GIANT

"ON THE OTHER SIDE OF THOSE TOWERING PEAKS, IN A LONG BASIN WHERE EVERGREEN FORESTS GROW THICKLY DOWN TO THE WHITE SAND OF SHORELINES, IS LAKE TAHOE. AND I AM REMINDED OF MARK TWAIN'S SAYING THAT THE CLEAR BLUE WATERS BLENDED SO WITH THE BLUE SKY OVERHEAD THAT A MAN IN A BOAT HAD THE SENSATION OF FLOATING IN AIR."
—ROBERT LAXALT

THE FABULOUS V & T

Frock coated William Sharon was a man who didn't mince words. He envisioned control of the Comstock and he needed a railroad to do it. Calling I. E. James to his office, he greeted the surveyor with a blunt question, "Can you build a railroad from Virginia City to the Carson River?" Equally as brief was James' reply, "Yes," and within a month the survey was completed and work commenced on the Virginia and Truckee Railroad, destined to become the most fabulous of all short lines.

Sharon represented the Bank of California, which in turn controlled a number of mills on the Carson River. Using bank credit as his trump card, Sharon was assured of ore for the mills since reduced freight rates would attract shipment of lean ore and even dump material. Timber for the Comstock deep mines was a constant commodity for the return haul.

Chinese workers, who learned construction on the Central Pacific Railroad, were imported to build the grade and lay the tracks for the V & T. Fearing cheap labor might invade the mining field, the miners' union drove the Asians from their camps and Sharon fumed for a week before he promised the union that the Chinese would never work the Comstock Mines. Work was resumed. Other uneasy moments occurred when the "Big Four" railroad Barons threatened to run a narrow gauge over Geiger grade connecting Virginia City with Reno, but Sharon was tenacious and the steel rails rapidly forged their way from Eagle Valley to the base of Sun Peak. In November of '69 they reached Gold Hill, two months later the first train rolled into Virginia City and the Comstock took a new lease on life.

Failing to compete with steam power, teamsters went out of business and the V & T hauled ore for two dollars a ton to the bank-controlled Union Mining and Milling Company mills on the Carson River. In '73 Mackay, Fair, Flood, and O'Brien hit their "Big Bonanza". The booming business necessitated an average of thirty trains a day over the twenty-one mile route between Carson and Virginia City. The peak haul was fifty-two trains a day. Railroaders worked a straight eighteen hours out of twenty-four, making four round trips daily. Sharon and his associates, Darius O. Mills and William C. Ralston split a hundred thousand dollars a month in dividends. The Comstock flourished, Julia Bullette was its reigning queen, fortunes were pyramiding and the V & T was the lifeline of commerce. Naturally it was a tempting morsel for holdups.

Today maintained as a tourist attraction, brass bound V & T engines appear regularly in motion pictures. The idol of railway associations, its yellow Kimball coaches once carried President Grant to the base of Sun Peak where he inspected the very mines that financed his Civil War campaigns.

STATE SEAL

Walker Lake (following page). Photograph by Roy Murphy.

erritoral status for Nevada was signed into law on March 2, 1861, a mere two days before Abraham Lincoln succeeded James Buchanan as President of the United States, this due in large measure to the discovery of the Comstock and ensueing population explosion, the threat of Civil War, and efforts of one die-hard Nevada lobbyist, J.J. Musser.

Boundaries set were most confusing, with the California line designated as the crest of the High Sierra, (subject to approval by that state's legislature) and only the border with Oregon and Idaho remaining unchanged to this day. Most of what became the territory of Nevada was extracted from Utah territory, virtually cutting the Mormon's "Empire" in half.

Seeing the need for another state partial to "Northern" sentiments, Lincoln wasted no time in establishing a fledging government. On March 22, he appointed James W. Nye of New York as governor, and one Orion Clemens of Iowa as secretary of the new territory. Clemens came west by stage accompanied by his younger brother Samuel (soon to become known to the world as Mark Twain).

Arriving in Carson City, designated seat of the new territorial government, Nye and Clemens proceeded to establish a government structure out of chaos. For the first time since the Mormon exodus law and order had arrived. The nominated legislators chose ironically as among their priorities to outlaw gambling by making it a felony (Nevadans saw to it that this eastern attempt at civility was soon overturned).

Endless Government sessions and silver strikes would best describe the decade that followed.

The July 4th constitutional convention of 1864, at a cost of more than $30,000, wired the whole of their freshly-drafted constitution to Washington by telegraph. Proclamation of statehood came on October 31st of that same year. The fact that the population of the entire territory numbered but 20,000 souls, one-sixth of the federal requirement for representation of the new state in Congress, was of minimal concern to Washington. Of far greater importance was the fact that the new state was producing millions of dollars a year in silver and gold. Thus the Silver State was born.

lections were held one week following Nevada's proclamation of statehood, after having spent less time than any other state, other than Alabama, between territorial status and statehood. It's newly appointed Senators, Nye and Stewart and congressman, H.G. Worthington, rushed off to Washington immediately so as to be able to cast their votes in favor of the 13th amendment to the Constitution of the United States.

Mining strikes continued. The establishment of the community of Ione led to the birth of camps at Grantsville, Berlin and Belmont. Arabia began, as did Candelaria. Strikes at Hamilton would kick off the White Pine County boom in

Nevada Gentry. While much of the riches from the Comstock flowed out of the territory some was invested in local ranching operations and elaborate homesteads.

A MINER'S BEST FRIEND, TODAY WILD BURROS ROAM NEVADA'S HIGH DESERT

1865 and lead to the birth of Eberhart, Treasure City, Shermantown, Cherry Creek, Mineral City, Osceola and Gold Creek before all its residents deserted Hamilton for Pioche in 1874.

Cattle had been introduced years earlier by Mormon settlers yet it was California ranchers that brought them enmasse to the state of Nevada, followed by sheep introduced by the Basques. Range wars were imminent in a land where good fodder was scarce and water precious.

The Transcontinental Railroad came over the Sierra and into Nevada in 1868. It muliplied the population and created a number of new towns- among them Reno, Elko, Lovelock, Wells, Battle Mountain and Wadsworth, and afforded ranchers a way by which to export Nevada beef to lucrative markets in both San Francisco and the East. Blessed by a thousand square miles of cattle and sheep ranches Nevada slipped easily into its role as a livestock capital.

The arrival of the Central Pacific Railroad also gave rise to a number of smaller, shortline railroads, the most famous of which was the opulent V & T (Virginia and Truckee) Railroad.

ROY MURPHY

Virginia City had grown to challenge even San Francisco in both population and extravagance, with Carson City and Reno riding to prominence on her coat tails.

In 1875 fire swept through the Queen of the Comstock, devouring more than half of the silver capitol. Always optimistic, Virginia City immediately rebuilt. Yet, by the end of the next decade the free flowing silver mines that seemed endless had infact begun to give out.

German and Italian immigrants had come to pursue agricultual enterprises, particularly in and around the Carson Valley area. As the mines began to play out, near the turn of the century, it was these agricultural and ranching enterprises that maintained an austere yet stable state economy.

By the early Twentieth Century all of Nevada slumbered, like a weary giant exhausted from his excesses. Yet the giant would awaken from that deep sleep to pursue an even more extravagant lifestyle. That awakening came slowly, at an all but imperceptible pace to even the most observant.

MAJOR MINING OPERATION (ABOVE) AT GOLD HILL

n an effort to bolster the state's sinking economy by promoting tourism, Reno proclaimed itself the home of championship prize fighting, a sport which in the best tradition of the West always resulted in a frenzy of gambling. This coupled by the fact that lenient divorce laws were attracting the rich and famous brought Nevada further notoriety. Scenic dude ranches, colorful cowboys and back-room gambling further enhanced the setting for that which was about to occur.

Mining continued, copper bonanzas and gold strikes — on again, off again — yet they were mere background noise for an unprecedented and completely unexpected "rebirth."

To counter the destructive effects of a nationwide depression and a lagging local economy, Nevada re-legalized gambling in 1931. A tradition in the mining camps on the Comstock, where the gambling hall went up just after the saloon and just before the dance hall, gaming (as Nevadans preferred to call it) had always been legal in the territory until reformers squelched it in 1910. Its subsequent rebirth did not go unnoticed by a nation which now considered its raucous wild-west traditions colorful and charming expressions of a youthful frontier long since past.

Former carnival promoter 'Pappy' Smith, in company with his two sons Raymond and Harold, set out to announce to the world that gaming was alive and well in Nevada. Setting up signs across the continent, tourists subsequently poured into their now famous 'Harold's Club' until four decades later it was sold to the Summa (Howard Hughes) Corporation for millions.

Meanwhile Bill Harrah proceeded to parlay a bingo game into an eighty- million dollar corporation to be traded on the New York Stock Exchange.

Jackie Vaughn and Sam Boyd pioneered gaming in Las Vegas with the opening of the El Rancho Vegas and El Cortez hotels in 1941.

An influx of Boulder (later Hoover) Dam workers fueled business in Vegas and a year later the Last Frontier Hotel was opened on a desolate stretch of desert destined to become today's world famous Las Vegas Strip.

8452 MILES TO RENO AND HAROLDS CLUB

t was the 1946 opening of a six million dollar Flamingo Hotel that permanently launched Las Vegas and Nevada itself into the bigtime, however, all of this secretly financed by outlaw Benjamin 'Bugsy' Siegel. Locals cringed when word leaked out about the underworld connection, yet who could argue with success.

As a result of all of this, a rather colorful and somewhat exaggerated folklore grew up about what by contemporary American standards was considered to be free-wheeling leniency.

A Nevada divorce became known as "the cure" or, by some, a "renovation." Tradition held that the newly liberated party must merely toss his or her wedding band into the waters of the Truckee River from the Virginia Street Bridge to "legally" consummate the transaction. It was reported in various newspaper columns throughout the country, and indeed

MUSTANGS

Horses roamed the new world prior to and during the Ice Age. They vanished however with the last of the glaciers only to be reintroduced to the continent some 7,500 years later courtesy of the Spanish conquistadores.

Subsequently the British, French and others brought with them other breeds as they explored and settled the Americas, many of which escaped to join errant Spanish stock in the wild. The result -a free- roaming, sturdy American breed less susceptible to disease and far more prolific than the more carefully bred domestic horses. By the dawning of the 20th century mustangs (from the Spanish ward mestengos) in the American outback were more numerous than the much touted 200,000 head heard of Australia.

Western ranchers recruited wild bands of mustangs as handy reserves of saddle stock and draft animals. Readily available, more serious collectors captured large numbers to supplement the cavalries of both American and European armies.

As the Industrial Revolutioned dethroned the horse, replacing it with machines, those of the open range became more valuable as dog food. By 1970 all but some 20,000 had been slaughtered.

Native Nevadan Velma Johnston, alias Wild Horse Annie, led the fight to save the last of the wild mustangs from her Reno home. Success followed when Congress enacted laws protecting this distincly American legacy. Their numbers have since tripled.

Today annual roundups conducted by the BLM (Bureau of Land Management) gather 8,000 animals to be offered up for adoption, thus carefully maintaining a stable, wild population.

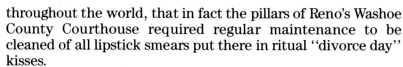

"NEVADANS KEEP INSIDE WHAT'S MEANT TO BE INSIDE. WE KNOW WHO WE ARE AND WHERE WE CAME FROM. SOME RESENT THAT. THEY WOULD RATHER SIT AROUND AND BOUNCE THEIR VIBES OFF EACH OTHER. THEY DON'T REALIZE THAT THEY'RE SUFFOCATING BECAUSE THEIR EMOTIONS HAVE NOWHERE TO GO. THEY DON'T KNOW WHAT IT IS TO GO OUT INTO THE LAND AND LET YOUR TROUBLES FLY AWAY INTO THE BIG SILENCE."

—*ROBERT LAXALT*

"YOU CANNOT LEGISLATE MORALS INTO PEOPLE, ANY MORE THAN YOU CAN LEGISLATE LOVE INTO THE HEARTS OF SOME PROFESSED CHRISTIANS. YOU CAN'T STOP GAMBLING, SO LET'S PUT IT OUT IN THE OPEN. DIVORCE IS THE ONLY SOLUTION WHEN MARRIAGES ARE UNHAPPY. AND IF I HAD MY WAY IN THIS PROHIBITION YEAR, I AS MAYOR OF RENO WOULD PLACE A BARREL OF WHISKEY ON EVERY CORNER, WITH A DIPPER, AND A SIGN SAYING: 'HELP YOURSELF, BUT DON'T BE A HOG.'"

—*MC CARREN*

72

throughout the world, that in fact the pillars of Reno's Washoe County Courthouse required regular maintenance to be cleaned of all lipstick smears put there in ritual "divorce day" kisses.

Further activities common to the American frontier (including the operation of brothels) were subsequently licensed by the State, bringing yet another source of revenue flooding into the Carson City coffers. More enlightened divorce laws since enacted by other states have considerably lessened the seeming liberalism of Nevada law. Gaming and the State's various other related interests remain yet unique. It is in fact this perpetuation of Wild West traditions that brought renewed economic stability and affluence to Nevada. All Nevadans, as well as the American economy itself, benefit from the ingenuity of the citizens of this still difficult Western territory.

Las Vegas subsequently boomed like a 19th century mining camp - its proximity to Los Angeles and Hollywood providing it with unlimited entertainment to headline acts for big money and a chance at the gaming tables.

Construction magnate Del Webb proceeded to expand upon his gaming empire, while billionaire Howard Hughes pumped millions into resort development (and mining operations) throughout the state. Fear of monopolies and continued infiltration by the underworld led to the establishment of controls under an appointed three man State Gaming Commission. Since that time the riotous growth of gaming parlors and casinos has been closely monitered. By 1975, gaming revenues topped a billion dollars, only to reach that level for Clark County (Las Vegas) alone by 1977.

Today there is nothing in all the world quite like Vegas. Foremost international gambling resort and home to over 600,000 people (among them many a show business superstar), Las Vegas plays host annually to more than 15 million people. Consequently, tourism/gaming remains the State's number one industry, mining 3.7 billion dollars in 1987; fueling another head-spinning, spiraling, economic bonanza to rival that of the Comstock itself.

Just beneath the surface of Nevada's sagebrush country precious metals lay everywhere, disseminated as microscopic particles throughout the State's entire geologic foundation. Considered too low grade to go after, with gold stuck at less than $35 an ounce, mining operations began anew in earnest as the precious metal soured to more than $400 an ounce on world markets. Today, due primarily to mining in Nevada, U.S. gold production ranks third in global output, behind South Africa and the U.S.S.R.

Trailing in third place, behind gaming/tourism and mining, huge water reclamation projects (such as that of the creation of Lake Lahonton near Fallon) have continued to bolster the State's agricultural base. Winnemucca with its potato crop, Fallon, renowned for its cantaloupes and watermelons, Genoa for its wheat, barley, turnips and yams, and everywhere rangeland ranching.

To further encourage industrial development the State of Nevada established itself as a Free Port with United States Customs facilities set up in both Reno and Las Vegas. Subsequently, warehousing for international corporations marketing to the western United States became a big business in the Silver State.

To further aid Nevada in establishing itself as *the* transportation and distribution center of western America favorable state tax laws were passed, encouraging additional investment. Today with an aggressive warehouse building and leasing industry in place, a strategic geographic location (in the heart of the Southwest adjacent to wealthy California) and an excellent transportation network, the entire region from Reno to Vegas has added yet another dynamic dimension to its burgeoning economy.

It was not until 1974 that Nevada achieved the population requirement usually represented by a United States congressman - 500,000 people. Carson City, with its silver-domed capitol building (smallest State Capitol in the 50 states), boasts a frontier elegance typical of Nevada. An independent city, today it governs 16 counties, with 85 percent of the State's million residents concentrated in booming Las Vegas and Reno.

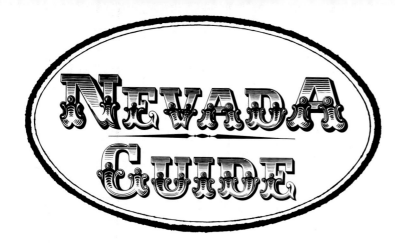

NEVADA GUIDE

rom the heady heights of Great Basin National Park to the desert shores of mammoth Lake Mead, Nevada continues to embrace the very essence of the American West. Here the old frontier lingers in friendly rural communities and relic ghost towns, while all that is the New West sparkles and shines amidst glamorous cities glittering in the incredibly vivid Nevada night sky.

Although one of the fastest growing states in America, Nevada yet remains the second most sparsely populated. Vast expanses of open space surround you no matter where you turn; the crowds and fast-paced tempo of Nevada's gaming resorts giving way almost immediately to the solitude and quiet of desert and mountain wilderness.

In the cities themselves new high-rise hotels, casinos, and office buildings contrast strikingly with surviving examples of Old West architecture. Beyond, such juxtapositioning of widely diverse elements is further expressed where muted tones of desert landscapes collide with vivid red rock country and the emerald verdure of spruce, fir, and pine in the high country.

Most of Nevada is located in a high desert region, where the climate encountered is arid. Temperatures can vary greatly depending upon altitude, ranging anywhere from 10 to 100 plus degrees Fahrenheit.

Las Vegas and Reno, at opposite ends of the silver state, offer all the amenities of any major American city plus the all-night gaming tradition of the Comstock that remains unique to Nevada territory.

It is in fact these elaborate world class gaming resorts that attract millions to Nevada each year. In Las Vegas the casino center downtown and the famous strip itself are lined with casino after casino, each vying for your attention with fabulous (and at times outrageous) marquees, architecture, and of course lights. The most elaborately lit city in the world it is in fact these lights that give Vegas in particular its all night aura of the fantastic.

Beyond the world-class casino resorts of Las Vegas lie a myriad of adventures to be indulged in.

Fueling the ravenous appetite for electricity of both Vegas and not so distant Southern California is gigantic Hoover Dam, one of the seven man-made wonders of the modern world. Constructed by an army of workers between 1931 and 1935, Hoover Dam today impounds yet another man-made wonder, Lake Mead, an aquatic wonderland in the middle of the desert.

Largest man-made body of water in the United States, with more than 550 miles of shoreline in its 115-mile length and

STATE FLAG

NEVADA's FIRST FLAG HAD A LEGAL LIFESPAN OF ONLY 10 YEARS AND WAS REPLACED IN 1915 BY A FLAG THAT INCLUDED THE STATE SEAL IN THE CENTER, SURROUNDED BY EIGHTEEN STARS.

IN L929, THE NEVADA LEGISLATURE APPROVED THE PRESENT STATE FLAG. THE DESIGN INCORPORATES A COBALT BLUE BACKGROUND WITH TWO SPRAYS OF SAGEBRUSH FORMING A HALF-WREATH AROUND A FIVE POINTED STAR IN THE UPPER LEFT CORNER. THE WORDS, "BATTLE BORN," ARE INSCRIBED ABOVE THE STAR, INDICATING THAT NEVADA BECAME A STATE DURING THE TURBULENT TIMES OF THE CIVIL WAR.

SHIMMERING LEAVES OF GOLD (preceding pages) Quaking Aspen greet the Fall traveler in Nevada's high country.

GOLFING IN LAS VEGAS

JAMES BLANK

THERE IS NOTHING IN ALL THE WORLD QUITE LIKE VEGAS, gaming capitol of the world. By day (photographs - these pages) Vegas Valley and environs cater to the sporting enthusiast and sightseer. As evening falls the muted desert tones and brilliant greens of this oasis give way to a spectacular show of lights. The ethereal beauty of Caesar's Palace at dusk (following page), one of many such resorts, is here transformed into a glitzy, glamorous nightime pleasuring ground.

HOOVER DAM

JAMES BLANK

DOWNTOWN VEGAS   JAMES BLANK

THE STRIP   JAMES BLANK

LAKE MEAD   MARK E. GIBSON

HOOVER DAM

covering an area of 229 square miles, Lake Mead is one of the major recreational attractions of the Southwest. More than six million people a year come here to enjoy boating, swimming, water-skiing and fishing (large mouth bass are the favorite here). Lake Mead is administered by the National Park Service.

Along the northern shores of Lake Mead lies the Valley of Fire State Park with its Lost City Museum. A 26,000-acre, open air archaelogical shrine to the Anasazi Indians of prehistoric Nevada, wind-chiseled sandstone formations and interesting Indian petroglyphs abound.

Magnificent Red Rock Canyon and the Spring Mountain Ranch are but a few miles west of Las Vegas. Here magnificent, brilliantly colored, mountains of sandstone rise above the beauty of a pristine desert landscape. An informative interpretive center enlightens visitors as to the wonderful variety of flora and fauna to be encountered here in the Mojave while at historic Spring Mountain Ranch tours of the main house are conducted on weekends and during holidays.

Only minutes beyond lies truly spectacular alpine scenery amidst the spruce and aspen draped slopes of Mt. Charleston in the Toiyabe National Forest. Picnic facilities, camping areas, and a fine lodge for wining and dining compliment this serene environment. Intrepid hikers may enter into ancient bristlecone forests and experience chance encounters with Rocky Mountain bighorn, elk, and muledeer. During the winter, Mt. Charleston's Lee Canyon affords an outstanding ski area for downhill runs.

In Las Vegas itself, one encounters a surprising number of cultural experiences. The Nevada State Museum, Las Vegas Museum of the Arts, Las Vegas Museum of Natural History (complete with life-size dinosaur replicas) and Old Tyme Gambling Museum (of course), are but a few of this community's offerings.

Five minutes from downtown Las Vegas is the Southern Nevada Zoological Park, featuring exhibits of extremely rare Barbary Apes and a large number of exotic bird displays, not to mention lions and tigers and bears.

Also a favorite is the Ethel M Chocolate Factory and Cactus Garden with its selfguided tour through outstanding examples of cacti, Southwest art, and, of course, chocolates.

At Bonnie Springs/Old Nevada, the re-creation of the Old West experience in a beautiful high desert setting is complete. Shops, rides, live gunfights, etc. make of this a favorite among the younger set.

Beyond, scenic highways lead off into the Arizona Desert with its incredible Grand Canyon of the Colorado and to Utah with its many National Parks.

Reno, today with a population approaching 250,000 proudly retains its accolade as "Biggest Little City in the World." On the grounds of its convention center stands the modest, yet stately mansion of the town's founder, Myron Lake, who established Reno as a preferred crossing (of the Truckee River) on the Old Emigrant Trail. Little could he have imagined that his settlement would wrest preeminance away from neighboring Virginia City, and yet that is precisely what transpired.

SKIING/LAKE TAHOE

SOUTH LAKE TAHOE   JAMES BLANK

WORLD FAMOUS HAROLD'S CLUB   MARK E. GIBSON

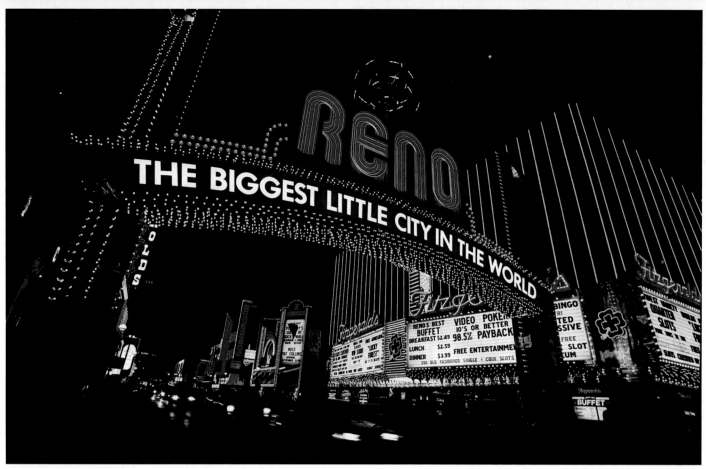

DOWNTOWN RENO

MARK GIBSON

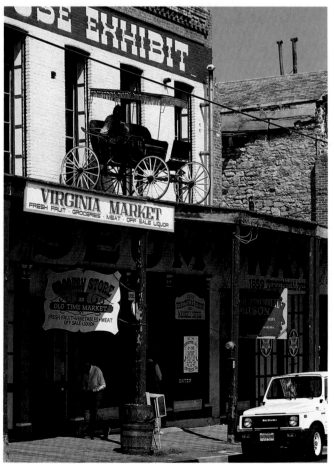

VIRGINIA CITY

JAMES BLANK

BIGGEST LITTLE CITY IN THE WORLD (photographs these pages) Reno today remains the commercial and historic center of the Silver State, with a nightlife to rival that of glamorous Las Vegas. Beyond, alpine splendor at Lake Tahoe and the rich frontier legacy of Virginia City further enhance this region of high desert and high mountains.

It was the coming of the railroads and their decision to place a depot at Reno, running tracks north of the Comstock Queen and thus dealing her a final fatal blow. Reno has ever since been the focal point of industrial development in Nevada; serving truly as the commercial epicenter of the Silver State.

Much like Vegas, and yet vastly more historic and different in geographic setting (glittering at the foot of the High Sierra) it was of course here in Reno that gaming was reborn, this during the 1930's. Today the pioneering Harrah's and Harold's Club share the spotlight with a score of other world class gaming resorts.

Downtown Reno, with its world famous arch and fabulously lit gaming casinos is a must see. Only slightly less ostentatious than those of Las Vegas they serve up a dining, gaming, entertainment, and shopping bill of fare that stands unequaled beyond Nevada. Harrah's also boasts the finest, most unique collection of vintage, antique, classic and special interest cars in the world. While Harold's Club sports a unique collection of rare firearms.

For the history buff Reno is a bonanza (in more ways than one). Adjacent to the University of Nevada is the intriguing Nevada Historical Museum and for the astronomer, the Fleischmann Planetarium.

In Washoe County's Rancho San Rafael Park, visitors can experience department store magnate Wilbur D. May's extensive Great Basin Museum and arboretum.

Elsewhere Reno's Sierra Nevada Museum of Art, housed in an elegant, historic Neo-Georgian mansion features noted works of the Great Basin region and 19th and 20th century American art.

South of Reno the history lesson continues with a visit to Virginia City. A walk down Front Street and visit to the mines conjures up the days when this was literally the richest city in the West. A ride on the fabulous V & T (Virginia and Truckee Railroad) will resurrect even more nostalgia.

And then of course there's Tahoe. Lake Tahoe's elegant resorts overlook the emerald beauty of America's most scenic alpine lake. Unparalleled facilities for both winter and summer sports abound as does the serenity and challenge of the High Sierra wilderness.

On the shores of Lake Tahoe is the Ponderosa Ranch, home to television's Cartwright family and "Bonanza," series (the most popular western of all times).

The Tram at Heavenly Valley Ski Resort affords spectacular views of the High Sierra during winter or summer while the U.S. Forest Service orients you to the flora, fauna, geology and history of the Sierra Nevada at its visitor center in South Lake Tahoe.

Vikingsholm Castle at Emerald Bay State Park is magnificent. The view from here is one of the most photographed scenes in the world.

MARK E. GIBSON

STATE BIRD

THE MOUNTAIN BLUEBIRD (SIALIA CURRUCOIDES) IS THE OFFICIAL NEVADA STATE BIRD. THE MALE IS AZURE BLUE WITH A WHITE BELLY AND VARIES BETWEEN SIX-AND-A-HALF AND SEVEN-AND-THREE-QUARTERS INCHES IN LENGTH. THE FEMALE IS BROWN WITH A BLUISH RUMP, TAIL AND WINGS. THE MOUNTAIN BLUEBIRD LIVES IN NEVADA'S HIGH COUNTRY AND FEEDS ON WILD FRUITS AND INSECT. IT IS A MEMBER OF THE THRUSH FAMILY AND ITS SONG IS A CLEAR SHORT WARBLE LIKE THE CAROLING OF A ROBIN.

"AT SUPPER THAT NIGHT, THE YOUNG COWBOY SUDDENLY TURNED PALE AND COULD NOT EAT. I FOLLOWED HIM OUTSIDE INTO THE FROZEN NIGHT AND ASKED HIM WHAT WAS THE MATTER. HE ANSWERED IN A VOICE TIGHT WITH STRAIN, 'I'VE GOT TO GO AWAY FROM HERE TOMORROW. TO THE ARMY. I'VE NEVER BEEN OUT THERE BEFORE.'
"WHAT HE DID NOT SAY, BUT I UNDERSTOOD, WAS THAT HE WAS ACTUALLY TERRIFIED. HE WAS ABOUT TO PAY THE PENALTY OF BEING REARED IN A SETTING OF ISOLATION. MY HEART WENT OUT TO HIM FOR WHAT HE WOULD SUFFER, BUT AFTER WHAT I HAD WITNESSED THAT AFTERNOON, I HAD NO FEARS ABOUT THE FACT THAT HE WOULD SURVIVE. WHAT HE DID NOT KNOW-AND I COULD NOT TELL HIM-WAS THAT THE LAND HAD ALREADY TAUGHT HIM THE LESSON OF ENDURANCE."
—ROBERT LAXALT

"SEEMS LIKE EVERYTHING'S AT LEAST HALF A WINDY DAY AWAY FROM EVERYTHING ELSE OUT THERE. SOMETIMES IT RANGES ON SO FREE AND ENDLESS I GET A COYOTE FEELING: I DON'T KNOW WHETHER TO SING FOR JOY OR CRY FOR MYSELF. WITH MY WINDOWS DOWN AND THE RADIO WAY UP AND ALL THE BLUE SKY IN THE WORLD OVERHEAD, I'M A 70-MILE-AN-HOUR PLUME OF DUST AND COUNTRY MUSIC ROLLING THROUGH A SILVER-GREEN SAGEBRUSH SEA."
—DOUGLAS H. CHADWICK
NATIONAL GEOGRAPHIC

Carson City, with its historic state capitol building, is another charming community full of beautiful Old West homes, antique shops and museums.

Picturesque and quaint Genoa, Nevada's oldest permanent settlement, is an excellent place to spend a quiet day strolling and exploring.

Stretching between Reno and Vegas is the Tonopah highway with its vast desert horizons and historic legacy of mining camps and cities. Of particular interest is Goldfield which still retains the ever declining ambiance of a onetime boom town. Tonopah itself serves as commercial epicenter for this region, while to the south Beatty services tourists as the gateway to the magnificent Death Valley National Monument.

Off the beaten path, at the end of countless, unmarked roads forever branching off from Nevada's highways, a hundred ghost towns dot the landscape.

Often referred to as the American Outback, Nevada is a country of far horizons broken only by mountain barriers lost in the haze of distance. Unexpected green valleys break upon the traveler's eye with the breath-stopping impact of a mirage. Meandering belts of greenery where giant cottonwoods and quaking aspen line the banks of streams and rivers that are as precious as gold in this land of little rain, divide and beautify the plains and deserts.

Situated in favored places there are quiet towns where water is plentiful and agricultural and or mining operations still flourish. Here buckaroos drive their cattle down from the summer range lands to winter pasture or market, school children sport cowboy boots and highways wander off into the forever reaches of purple pine-crested mountains and sage covered plains to distant ranches. From Elko to Winnemucca and beyond, the traditional American West lives here in the lives and businesses of Nevada's ranchers and farmers. A trip into the interior affords one an opportunity to experience this true West.

In Elko, heart of Nevada's "cattle country" and gateway to some of the State's most scenic mountain country is the Northeastern Nevada Museum with its fine displays which include an actual Pony Express Way Station.

Towns such as LaMoille, Wells, McDermitt and Battle Mountain, like countless other Nevada communities, each possess a charm unique to the West.

Along U.S. Highway 50, reputedly the "Loneliest Road in America", one encounters the one-time copper mining center of Ely, today's gateway to nearby Great Basin National Park, a splendid stretch of mountain and desert wilderness, subterranean caverns and ancient bristlecone forests.

In sharp contrast to tiny Baker and historic Pioche, communities such as Jackpot and Laughlin offer the raucous clatter of slot machines and the scintillating lights of the casino.

Nevada then, in brief summation, embraces the traditions of the old and the opportunities of the new West, boldly positioned today at the dawning of the Twenty-first century.

 EPILOGUE

Until the letter caught up with me, I had taken Nevada pretty much for granted. I suppose that attitude was a normal one for youth who have known only one setting from the time of first awareness until the circumstance of war catapults then across a continent and an ocean and deposits them in an alien land.

So it was with me. The letter was from a friend in Nevada. That much I noticed. But I was only vaguely aware that there seemed to be something more than paper inside. When I was alone, I opened the envelope. With the unsealing came the unleashing of a forgotten scent that struck me like a physical force.

Hidden between the pages was a single sprig of Nevada sagebrush. Before I could protect myself, the memories were summoned up and washed over me in a flood. They all had to do with sagebrush.

Sagebrush that rolled over the vast plateaus and brutal desert mountains like an endless gray sea, ringing the few scattered hamlets and towns of Nevada so that they were like islands in that sea. Sagebrush growing down to the banks of rare streams and rivers so that water seemed to be captive in a bigger sea. Sagebrush giving up its domain only when it reached the foothills of the western Sierra where deep forests of pine and fir and tamarack ruled supreme.

Sagebrush in the spring with the tender tips of first growth mingling with the gray. Sagebrush in the summer when the blazing sun made the scent almost unbearably pungent. Sagebrush after a spring rain when that scent was muted to the heady fragrance of wine. Sagebrush in the autumn when golden pods burst into puffs at the mere touch of a hand. Sagebrush in the winter, hooded white with snow so that

walking through it was like walking through a gnome forest.

The smell of a sagebrush cookfire at dusk in a desert hollow that was bedground for our sheep, shaggy sheepdogs resting in its light and warmth, and the indistinct figure of my father saying that sagebrush made the hottest cookfire one could ask for. A tobacco-chewing prospector with a stained mouth and a face so scarred by sun and wind that his wrinkles were like black ravines in his flesh, stopping by for coffee out of a blackened pot, while his overloaded burro waited with hanging head until he could be relieved of a burden made impossible by a hundred pieces of promising rock. A buckaroo with a big hat and built-up heels on his way home to the ranch at end of day, his powerful horse plowing through the sagebrush as if it were an enemy. The Paiute Indian boys of my childhood running with fluid motion through an unbroken tangle of sagebrush without even breaking their stride, because sagebrush was in their blood and bones, and their familiarity with it was drawn down from uncounted generations who had hunted there before the first white man had dared venture into the unknown land.

Since that long-ago day when a single sprig of sagebrush brought Nevada home to me, I have taken her no more for granted. Always when I return, one of the first things I must do is go out into the sagebrush until its chemistry works in me and I know I am home again. But now, older, I find myself reflecting whimsically on how very much like the sagebrush the people are, at least in the hinterland that makes up the most of Nevada, setting down roots and thriving in unlikely places, hardy and resilient, stubborn and independent, restrained by environment and yet able to grow free.

--Robert Laxalt

"Nevada - A Bicentennial History"
published by W.W. Norton &
Company, Inc. ©1977

INDEX

Type in boldface indicates photographer or illustration

ACKNOWLEDGEMENTS

No project as involved as the production and publication of a new book is ever completed without the contributions of time and talent from many dedicated individuals. NEVEDA - THE SILVER STATE is the result of just such an effort.

We wish to express our appreciation to each anonymously for his or her generous assistance and scholarly adivce — to photographers and illustrators who have remained supportive throughout the years — to production and backup staff — and to Divine providence always.

ADAM RANDOLPH COLLINGS
incorporated